CW00499047

My Fourpenny Jesus

Poems and pieces by

by

Margaret Randall

Hanover Books

FOURPENNY JESUS contains works of fiction.
Any similarity to actual persons or events is
purely coincidental.

Copyright © Margaret Randall 2011

Margaret Randall asserts the moral right to be
identified as the author of this work.

ISBN 978-1-907897-01-6

Published by Hanover Books
www.hanoverbooks.co.uk

All rights reserved. No part of this publication may be
reproduced, stored in a retrieval system, or transmitted,
in any form or by any means, electronic, mechanical,
photocopying, recording or otherwise, without the prior
permission of the publishers.

THANKS

With grateful thanks to Stan and his computer

CONTENTS

All God's People

Spare A Prayer For The Animals

Remembering

Happy Thoughts

Family and Friends

You Raise Me Up

INTRODUCTION

What has happened to our lovely England? This isn't the England I remember of my childhood. Recently in the newspaper I read that a woman picked up a kitten, dropped it into a wheelie-bin and walked calmly away leaving it to its fate. No, this isn't my England anymore.

I remember so well my schooldays, when our first lesson in the morning was Scripture and we were taught to care about our friends and neighbours and always be kind, especially to animals. After that we studied the three "R"s, reading, writing and arithmetic. Now many of our children leave school without even learning to read and write. What has gone wrong?

As a child I was a dreamer and spent a lot of time on my own making up stories and poems. Writing was the only thing I was any good at. But schooldays came to an abrupt end for me, when at the tender age of twelve my beloved father died and our home was destroyed in the Blitz. It affected our family very badly. My mother, brothers and I were broken hearted and felt like giving up but as Winston Churchill would have advised at the time, we just had to carry on like "good soldiers".

Later, with both brothers married, there was only Mum and me, quietly content and settled now that the war was over. I got work as a kennel maid at Walthamstow Greyhound Stadium. Not being academic but loving animals, this job suited me. My best friend Doreen came to work there too, so it was ideal. And I still kept on with my scribbling.

Then, through taking a writing magazine, I became a pen pal with John Randall who lived in Reading. After corresponding for some time and exchanging photographs we arranged to meet under the clock at

Victoria Station. We had already learned a lot about each other through our writing so we were at ease immediately and our friendship soon blossomed into love (which lasted over forty years).

Throughout the years I attended Islingwood Road Church. It was at this church one Sunday morning that I realised how much I was blessed. Our Pastor Peter King invited anyone who wanted to feel nearer the Holy Spirit to come forward to the altar. A few others and I did so and Peter prayed earnestly for us. Some people in the congregation stood behind us in case we were to fall. I'd heard this could happen but didn't think it would happen to me. However, as Peter prayed for us, a most beautiful peaceful feeling went through my whole body. It was just like I imagined being in Heaven would feel. I don't know how long I was "suspended" there but finally I found myself floating like a feather to the ground. Someone came to help me up but I just wanted to stay where I was, within that wonderful experience.

Many years later John became ill with Parkinson Disease which brought hard times for us (almost 16 years). Yet in spite of it all we managed to stay happy together and I know it was because Jesus was helping us through the good times and, more importantly, the bad. I began writing poetry again. Mostly inspirational pieces and animal poems. I used to read them out to John and he'd smile and sometimes nod his head in approval.

This book has made it possible for me to get all my writing together inside one cover. As you may see, I've tried to get "a little bit of Jesus" into all my work. I hope you will find it and that it will meet with your approval.

From Margaret
With love

Poems and Pieces

A POEM THAT RHYMES

I like a poem that rhymes
......one you can "sing" like a song,
A poem that gives a message of hope
And carries its tune all along.

It might tell of the wonderful sea
'Til you feel the salt spray on your face
Or set you up high on top of a hill
Without even the labour of pace.

A poem when you're feeling low
Can "jog" you along with a smile
Using its "sing-songy" words
To charm and amuse and beguile.

It can paint you a picture that soothes
As its colours drift into your mind
With pastels of mauves, pinks and blues
The proverbial Rainbow you'll find.

It can show you a beautiful scene
Of a baby on fond mother's knee
With a face full of love......so serene
That glimpses of heaven you'll see.

Not for me any terse modern verse
With issues of these troubled times
Give me the melodious lilt
Of an old-fashioned poem that rhymes.

OUR FOUR SEASONS

Spring so sweetly rains
Her fragrant April showers
So that each glade and glen
Is carpeted with flowers.

Summer runs barefoot
Blue ribbon in her hair
She wears a golden dress
That touches everywhere.

Autumn spreads her seed
Till all the earth's abrim
With God's gold harvest gifts
To safely gather in.

Winter holds my hand
And breathes upon my face
And gives each naked tree
A negligee of lace.

WINTER'S PINAFORE

Winter stood at Autumn's gate
A spray of snowdrops in her hand
Eager to curtail her wait
And tiptoe o'er her sister's land.
But Autumn smiled and shook her head
Of golden tresses Heaven met.
"Oh no dear sister……no", she said,
"It isn't time for you……not yet".
And then with beauty in her heart
She sang and danced in splendid style,
Reluctant of her charms to part
To suit her sister's anxious wile.
But soon she slept and kept God's law
'Neath Winter's snow-white pinafore.

THE REASON

I often wonder "why" Lord
I'm here upon the earth.
I often wonder "if" Lord,
I'm here to prove my worth.

When problems come upon me
……Like hard times or ill health
It isn't until then Lord
I recognise my wealth.

For you are always with me
To lead along the way
It's up to me to listen
To follow and obey.

You'll help me face the bad things
And make of them the best.
Then I will know when life is through
I haven't failed the test.

MY PATCHWORK QUILT

The lovely patchwork quilt you see
Now lying on my bed
With cosiness will cover me
When I lay down my head.
My friend picked out the different wools
And patiently she built
A pattern that's a joy to see
My lovely patchwork quilt.
Each time I go into my room
It fills me with good cheer
I'd rather have that patchwork quilt
Than one of silken sheer.
It's squares of crochet......pinks and blues
Thrill me to the hilt,
So thank you friend for making me
My lovely patchwork quilt.

TEMPER

The day had gone badly
Sharp words had been said.
Tempers had flared up
And come to a head.

And yet when we'd finished
And tempers were spent
It was such a small item
That caused the event.

So don't let us quarrel
It'll get us nowhere.
It might cost us our friendship
And make us despair.

Let's settle our differences
And each other forgive
For the lower our blood pressure
The longer we'll live.

THE DREAMERS

Let us keep the Dreamers for they are like jewels
upon the earth
With their beauty misted eyes they see beauty
everywhere
We'll keep the Dreamers......they are rare.

Let us keep the Dreamers for they are more precious
than you think
With their pure and high ideals and angel thoughts
to share.
Help the Dreamers......they are rare.

Let us love the Dreamers for they can walk in squalor
yet see the sun
With their goodness of soul and
benevolence fair
We'll love the Dreamers......they are rare.

NEVER ALONE

Although my parents were kind and wonderful people, well respected by everyone, they were not churchgoers except for weddings and funerals, so I rarely saw the inside of a church and was never made to go to Sunday School.

Yet somehow, right from childhood, I felt someone was watching over me. But it wasn't until I started school and began Scripture lessons (always first lesson in the morning) that I realised that "Someone" was my Jesus.

Our elderly teacher painted such a colourful picture of this wonderful man Jesus that I took Him to my heart and He has been there ever since.

On Saturday mornings Mum and I always went shopping in Walthamstow High Street and we'd have a lovely time raking around the market stalls. One Saturday I found a small plastic figure of Jesus. He had come off His cross and I bought Him for four old pennies. When I got home Dad set Him on a little wooden Cross for me and I took that cross everywhere, especially down in to the air raid shelter, for we were in the middle of the war years at that time.

Eventually one night a bomb dropped on the house opposite us and we were made homeless. Everyone was upset, crying and screaming but we managed to scramble to safety out of the Anderson Shelter (cat and all) without any of us being hurt. Smugly I held on to my little cross-for I knew it was my Jesus who saved us that awful night. I still have that Cross hanging on the wall beside my bed today.

* * * * *

Much later in life I made pen pals with John. We were both interested in writing and poetry. Eventually John became my husband. Unfortunately we couldn't get

married in a church because John had been married some years before and in those days churches wouldn't allow second marriages, so we were married in a Registry Office.

From the start things were difficult. It wasn't easy to find somewhere to live and we didn't have much money......so we embarked on a care-taking way of life. We managed to get a beautiful basement flat in Diocesan Church House, Brunswick Square, where we were responsible for looking after the church offices and the security of the building. John continued his job as insurance man and helped me with the cleaning at the weekends.

There was a lovely chapel within the premises, which I grew to love, and where I took Holy Communion every Thursday morning. Then one day someone asked me where I had been baptized. I remember the look of horror on their face when I replied I hadn't. I was told gently but firmly that I shouldn't partake in Communion until I was. Immediately I arranged for the Rev. A. N. Evans of our local St. Andrews Church, Waterloo Street to baptize me. After that I attended St. Andrews and was confirmed at All Saints. The Rev. Evans and I became good friends and I always thought of him as a man with one foot in Heaven.

John and I lived and worked happily at Church House for twelve years, although unfortunately I was never able to get him to go to church with me.

Suddenly, though, it was decided that the whole inside of Church House was to be altered. Offices were re-constructed to make extra offices and the elegant doors and banisters were taken away to make room for fire doors. Even my beloved Chapel was re-located and the inside of the beautiful old house was changed beyond recognition.

Whilst all this work was being done, it was like living on a building site and impossible to keep clean. We decided (after much prayer on my part) that enough was

enough and we would look for another home. Finally we were able to purchase on mortgage a small flat in Kemp Town.

We liked living in Kemp Town and were there almost ten years. We had not been blessed with children but we both worked at St. Dunstans and got involved with the care of the blind ex-servicemen and women. I looked after the women's wing. Some of them had been blinded and maimed in the munitions factories and forces.

What an inspiration these women were to me; it was unbelievable what some of them had been through and how cheerful they managed to keep. Most of them possessed a deep inner strength and told me that God was always with them at their worst times. I could empathise with that.

My Jesus had always done the same for me, although I had never suffered like those poor women had.

However, problems soon arose. I developed very painful arthritis because of a fall some years before. I could no longer work at St. Dunstans and was incapacitated for two years, having to spend a lot of time laying flat on my back. I don't know how I would have managed without John, Doreen (my old school friend) and of course, my faith in Jesus. Thankfully and prayerfully my health gradually improved. I was able to get a part-time job as a sales assistant in a shop. The people I worked for became valued friends and are still so today.

The next blow came when John was diagnosed as having Parkinsons Disease. We couldn't believe it at first as it started with such minute symptoms......but it's one of those illnesses that soon progresses and in the end he had to give up his job. Now we could no longer afford the maintenance of our Kemp Town flat so were forced to sell it for a meager sum, which was not enough to buy another place to live.

Soon we were back in the care-taking life, only this time the work was wholly my responsibility......but with

God's help things ran smoothly for a time.

Then John's condition worsened and he was confined to a wheelchair. Now I was at my wits' end. I just couldn't manage the care-taking and looking after John at the same time.

I put our names down on a couple of Housing Association lists and prayed hard for a small one-bedroom flat that I could manage more easily. Up to now we had always lived in older accommodation that was harder to keep clean. I even had the cheek to ask Jesus for a "new modern labour saving place". Thankfully our prayers were answered and strangely it was the Diocesan Housing Association that came to our rescue...... and best of all, the new flat they offered was built within the walls of St. Wilfrid's Church, Elm Grove that had been derelict for some years. So we were virtually living within church walls with the bonus of having a large golden cross set in the brickwork just above our heads. This seemed like a miracle to me and I felt truly blessed.

Time went on and soon John could hardly do anything for himself. He was a wonderful patient and never complained but all the lifting was playing havoc with my back and we were both getting very low in spirit. John spent some time in hospital just to give me a rest but he was so unhappy there I arranged with Social Services to get a hospital bed and a hoist installed in our home.

With the help of wonderful nurses and carers I managed as best I could. Because I couldn't get out I began writing poetry again and was lucky enough to get them accepted by Age Concern, who also produced a small booklet of my work, all proceeds going to them.

Now John could no longer write or speak. That broke my heart for being a Welshman he had loved singing and had a beautiful tenor voice. He'd been a member of the Crescent Operatic Company......but now he couldn't even say my name.

Many times I was driven to distraction and cried out for our Lord's help. I began attending Islingwood Road Immanuel Church on Sunday mornings, leaving John safely tucked up in bed. I knew he was pleased for me to get some spiritual help there from my Church friends and Pastor Peter King. Peter started visiting John at home and became a valued friend and John was happy to let Peter pray for him.

When John died it was Peter King who got me through the terrible time at the hospital. He arranged for Doreen (my old school friend) to be with me and helped me when I had to make the heart-breaking decision not to let John be resuscitated.

Peter took John's funeral at the Downs Crematorium and an excellent job he made of it. If I were to say I was distraught with grief, I would not be telling the truth. It was as if a great weight lifted from me. I miss John of course, (we had been married over forty years) but it is a relief and blessing not to have to see him suffering any more.

Our Church in Islingwood Road was burnt down in 2001 and was a great loss to the people who worshipped there. I have now become a member of the Salvation Army (an organisation that my parents held in great esteem although they weren't churchgoers). I regard myself as a very fortunate person, having so many kind and loving people in my life, not least Doreen, my dear old school friend of over seventy years. She is the sister I never had and we are closer today than ever.

Although I live alone, I am never lonely for Jesus is always in my heart.

I truly believe that God is looking after my John and my wonderful parents and I'm sure that one day we will all be together within the beautiful spirit of our dear Lord, Jesus Christ.

Thank you God.

Christian Inspiration

An Easter Prayer

A BYSTANDER

It's Friday Lord and there you are
Still hanging on the cross.
How can I, standing here below,
Accept such daunting loss?

I do not know as I wait here
How long the time will be
Before they come and cut you down
And you'll disappear from me.

I gaze upon your tortured face
Your wounds are flowing now
I watch your life's blood drain away
Oh Lord......please use your power.

To rise up from the cruel cross
So I, who wait, can see
You truly are my saviour Lord
And you have died for me.

But wait......too late, tormentors come
To scoff and put you down
They laugh and jeer and throw away
The thorns that made your crown.

He called Himself the King of Jews
One laughing soldier said
No longer now the "King of Jews"
The King of Jews is dead.

I turn away, I cannot stay
There's tempest all around
The earth is crumbling 'neath my feet
My Lord has let me down.

I flee into my humble home
To find a place to weep
And finally I shut my eyes
And lose my pain in sleep.

But now 'tis Monday, and I rise
I have my chores to do.
Yet hopelessness is in my heart
For my saviour wasn't true.

I step out on the road and see
A man in robes of white
He stretches out his hands to me
And then I see the light.

"Come with me my child", he says
"Why did you not believe?"
"My prophecies have all come true
Not once did I deceive.

I am the Way, the Truth, the Life
These things are of accord
I am the saviour of your soul
I am the risen Lord

A Prayer

TRULY I AM THY SERVANT

Dear Lord, help me to serve you
Help me to know the desires of your heart
So that I can take up your cross and follow.

How much you must suffer when you see our sins
How much you must grieve that we are such
Disobedient children.

Let me dear Lord, kneel at your feet
To loosen your sandals and bathe each
Precious foot with love and devotion
And so ease away the sins of the world

BLESSINGS

When we are hurt Lord, you dry our tears
When we are troubled you soothe us
When we are frightened, you quell our fears
When we are angry you calm us

When we are sad Lord, you lift our hearts
When we feel poorly you heal us
When we lose hope, you give us faith
When we do wrong you forgive us.

BELIEVE

I've heard people say they could never "believe"
As the world is so wicked today.
They blame all their ills and bad fortune on God
……and laugh when you urge them to pray.

They don't see the wonderful beauty of life
The magnificent skies and the sea.
They only rejoice in what money can buy
And reject what God's given us…free.

They don't seem to hear the sweet sound of birds
Or see the gold sunsets at night.
So many good things God's given to us
……and all for our joy and delight.

Most bad things begin because of man's greed,
Always wanting more wealth and more power,
With never a care for what harm may be caused
As long as the goal's reached somehow.

But who do we call on when danger is near
Our very souls rise to Him then.
"Please help me God", are the first words we say
"Please help me God"……and amen.

YOUR FOOTPRINTS

Dear Lord,

I have read that lovely prayer - FOOTPRINTS, where you carry me through the tempests of life - one day Lord, when my life on earth is over, would that I could put my feet into those dear footprints of yours and walk within your perfect shadow and be as one with the Holy Spirit.

Amen.

YOU LORD

If I didn't have you Lord, who would there be
To sort out my problems and look after me?
How would I manage to face every day,
To recharge my batteries and go on my way?

It's only because Lord, I know you are there
I can hold up my head and keep from despair
And you'll never leave me, I know that is so
For your spirit is with me, wherever I go.

DEAR LORD

Dear Lord, I'm in a sorry plight
I don't know what to do
I've tried to manage on my own
But now I'm calling you.

Please will you calm and comfort me
So when I sleep tonight
You'll heal me with your loving grace
And help me put things right

I always try to do my best
But sometimes things go wrong
It's then I really need you Lord
To carry me along.

Now I've had these words with you
My mind is more at rest
I'm feeling so much better Lord
I'm feeling really blessed.

It's true what that dear poem says
Of "footprints in the sand"
I now see just one set of prints
And truly understand.

A LITTLE BIT OF JESUS

There's a little bit of Jesus
In everyone we meet
So let us try to remember this
When next a soul we greet.

We know that human beings
Are a mixture ......good and bad
But if we seek to find the good
The good's there to be had.

All of us can make mistakes
It's not for us to judge
We can only keep our faith
And try to show our love.

For God has given all a chance
By sending down His Son
To spread the beauty of His soul
And enrich us, everyone.

So if we try to live God's way
Our lives can be made sweet
For there's a little bit of Jesus
In everyone we meet.

WITHOUT YOU LORD

What would I do without you Lord?
How could I face every day
If I didn't feel you close by my side
To hear me whenever I pray?

How could I manage the turmoil of life
Without patience and guidance from you?
All on my own I'd flounder and fall
......I just wouldn't know what to do.

But you lift me up and keep my head high
You fill me with hope and delight
And make me aware of the blessings I have
Which sometimes get hidden from sight.

So I'll never walk without you Lord
I'll keep my faith constant and true
Safe in the knowledge that I needn't fear
As long as I journey with you.

CARES

Take your cares to Jesus
He will see you through
Your trials and tribulations
And things that worry you.
Let His arms uplift you
And fold you to His breast
Leave your cares with Jesus
He knows what is best.

APOLOGIES TO THE LORD

Lord I know that I didn't choose you but you chose me.
You have given me my life so you know my weaknesses and temptations.
You already have a blueprint of my life and know the way I should live it - but it is up to me to fashion each step so that it unfolds to your liking.
I pray Lord, that out of the pitfalls and difficulties that beset me, I can make something worthwhile which will please you.
So Lord, if I have not done things the way you meant me to - please forgive me.
If I have missed a chance of doing an act of kindness - please forgive me.
If I have been thoughtless and uncaring to any of my brothers and sisters - please forgive me.
But most of all Lord, if I have offended and disappointed you, I am truly sorry
- please forgive me.

MY FOURPENNY JESUS

I don't know why I picked Him from the squalor of old Ozzie's bric-a-brac stall. It might have been because I'd just moved up to the junior school and our first lesson of the day always started with Religious Instruction. Our kindly scripture teacher, Miss Scrutton, had begun telling us the story of Jesus. I was so intrigued and entranced by the picture she painted of this wonderful man that when I saw the small plastic figure of Him amongst the tangled mass of old glass beads and curtain rings on the stall, something made me pluck Him up and hold Him tight in my hand.

On closer inspection, He was a sorry sight. His feet were clamped one on top of the other with a nail mark driven through. His head drooped despondently to one side and His thin arms were stretched horizontally with hands palm uppermost. Holes were plainly visible in both where they had once been nailed to the now non-existent Cross.

"Please Sir, how much?" I asked old Ozzie. His curly eyebrows rose in surprise. "Err.....give me fourpence," he sniffed.

My heart sank. That was twice my week's pocket money and money was short in our household in 1939, just before War broke out. But all was not lost for my Mother, who I was accompanying on our usual Saturday morning mooch around the market, was standing nearby.

"Mum, could you lend me......?" I must have looked

up at her with such pleading eyes that she sensed how desperately I wanted the plastic Jesus - and she knew by my expression I wasn't going to give in without a fuss.

"What do you want it for?" she asked "it's broken and dirty and it's come off its cross."

"But it's Jesus Mum......and I can clean Him up, and Dad will make me a wooden cross to hang Him on."

Mum smiled. She was a lovely Mum, but neither she nor my Dad were what you would call religious. They never went to Church or made me and my brother go to Sunday school. But they were good "salt of the earth" type people; always ready to help anyone in trouble.

Needless to say I was able to pay old Ozzie the fourpence and happily carry the plastic Jesus carefully and reverently home. Taking great care, I cleaned Him up as gently as I could for He was very fragile. Dad made me a small wooden cross; he even varnished it and set Jesus upon it... although I couldn't bear to watch when he tapped the nails in.

In 1940 when the Battle of Britain started, the little cross went with me every night into the Morrison shelter. Morrisons, (named after Herbert Morrison the Home Secretary) were indoor shelters, little more than glorified kitchen tables but made of the strongest, toughest steel. Underneath we would go, my mother, brother and I (and sometimes the family cat), sleeping head to toe like sardines in a tin and covering our ears against the thudding of Mr Hilter's bombs.

Father wasn't with us because he had to do his duties at Liverpool Street Station in the heart of London and only came home in the early mornings. I think he was quite relieved that he didn't have to duck under the Morrison with us......and the cat.

Later in the war, when the doodle bugs arrived on the scene, we managed to get an Anderson shelter dug into our tiny back yard. My brother painted a name sign for it "Dew Drop Inn" and propped it up over the doorway. The Anderson was much more comfortable, even

though it was usually ankle deep in water. We had bunks fixed up in it and I can remember sitting on mine, with the plastic Jesus clutched tightly in my hand as the Doodle Bugs droned ominously overhead.

The time to worry was when their engines cut off - then everyone sat with heart in mouth ‘til the bomb landed somewhere. Of course we were always full of sympathy for the poor people on the receiving end, yet at the same time hoping fervently that it wouldn’t be our turn next. However I don’t remember ever feeling too afraid, for didn’t I have my little four penny Jesus to keep me and all the family safe?

I’m a pensioner now. I’ve had several different homes in my lifetime, and my plastic Jesus has been with me in every one; usually hanging somewhere close to the head of my bed where I can see Him - and He can see me.

He is a very precious possession although He only cost four pence in old money. To me He represents my Mother and Father - and my Heavenly Father. I wouldn’t part with Him for anything in the World.

My Fourpenny Jesus was first published in
This England magazine, *Spring 2002*

All God's People

HIS TREE

They had come to fell his tree,
The one where all his summers had been spent,
Where he had fixed a swing on branches kindly bent.
And now they had come with axes raised in zest
To execute the thing that he loved best.

But what cared they? For they had long forgot,
The boyish games that once they too had played
Midst leafy boughs, similarly made
And now they'd come to make a boy's tears start,
To fell the tree, deep rooted in his heart.

I MET A MAN......

I met a man...... along the street
He had no shoes upon his feet
His hair was long, his beard unkempt

Not a person to select
...more a person to reject!

Yet something in him made me pause
Although I didn't know the cause
With jacket torn......and trousers worn
His whole appearance was forlorn.

But then he looked at me and smiled
And right away I was beguiled
By two kind eyes, so meek and mild.

It made me think of long ago
Another man I used to know
When Sunday School I had to go.

He had a beard and long dark hair
His feet were strong and brown and bare
......though sometimes sandals he would wear.

Not a person to reject
......more a person to select......Jesus.

DOWN AND OUT

After seeing a poor man laying prone on a bench in the middle of Brighton, with a couple of empty beer cans by his side, I couldn't help but wonder what had happened in his life to make him reach this point? It made me count my blessings and think, "There but for the Grace of God go I".

They won't let me sleep in the park.
I've tried but they just move me on.
It's as if I'm not fit to be seen -
as if I've done something wrong.
Yet in my life I have tried to be fair
and once had a wife and two kids,
until she found comfort elsewhere
and then I was soon on the skids.
I got in with a hard drinking crowd
and soon just drank to forget -
forgetting I'd once been so proud
I let myself get into debt.
I soon lost my job and my home;
my friends turned away in disgust.
Now I feel so completely alone
with no one to love or to trust.
I do try to keep myself clean
for I know I offend people's eye.
They don't know the man I have been
when they shudder and quickly pass by.
They don't know that when I was young,
I saved a young child from the sea.

My deed went unnoticed, unsung
but that didn't matter you see.
For I had been taught to be good
and help any soul in distress,
but after what's happened to me
I fear I have sadly regressed.
So now I have only one hope:
that God in his wisdom will see
that under this poor outer shell
There's a person of worth - who is me.

NELL

I've written a few poems for "Age Concern", who were kind enough to produce an anthology of my work called "Poems & Pieces". I've incorporated most of them, as well as "Nell", into this book.

She sits in the park in her old hat and coat
And remembers her youth long ago
She didn't know then how life would turn out
......what pleasure and sorrows would flow.

She'd been christened Helen, a nice enough name
But most people knew her as "Nell".
It was "Nell do this" and "Nell do that"
And good hearted she did it all......well.

But now as she sits lost deep in thought
People don't notice her much
They don't know that once she'd been a young bride
Treasured......and very much loved.

She'd had seven children......her and her "Will"
But where are those children today?
They're married and scattered all over the world
And "Will"......he has long passed away.

Yes - She's met all life's battles and
"fought the good fight"
And now she is sitting alone
Patiently waiting - quietly content
'Til God calls... "Well done Nell... Come home."

POEM FOR A NEW BABY

Thank you gentle Jesus
For leaving in our care
This perfect little angel
For angels are so rare.

We'll try to always keep her
Safe within our love,
Knowing you'll be there Lord
......watching from above.

Please let your perfect spirit
Shine upon her face
And fill her life with beauty
......happiness and grace.

Grant our darling daughter
The joys a good life brings
For she's so very precious
......our angel without wings.

THE BLIND MAN

I spoke to a blind man… I asked him if he
Still longed for his sight? … He said this to me:

"I know the beauty and feather of touch,
The sound and the spray of the sea.
I know by instinct the presence of good,
My darkness is well lit for me.
I know the lines of a face when it smiles,
The tune of a voice when it speaks.
A friend is close by to show me the way
Whenever my outstretched hand seeks".

I said to the blind man… you've made plain to me,
How clearly the sightless can see.

THE MIGHTY ARTIST

Have you seen a picture of a country road
Where a man is labouring 'neath a heavy load?
Would you not have helped him
Had you been there too
Painted on the canvas in your coat of Prussian blue?

Have you seen a road in life, similar maybe,
Where a man is stumbling, lost in misery?
What's to stop you stepping
Through that canvas square
What's to stop you shouldering
Some of that man's care?
But quick, for chance like varnish
Will dry 'neath evening's blush
And soon the Mighty Artist may lay aside his brush.

TRUE FRIENDS

Friends feel for each other
On all occasions they are there for each other
Remembering birthdays and all special days
Ever thoughtful, in all kinds of ways.
Very sympathetic when things go wrong
Even to the end, they are staunch and strong.
Remember these qualities make a true friend.

Friends share good times and help in bad
Rallying around when you're feeling sad.
Instinctively knowing the right thing to say
Even when black clouds diminish your day.
Never take for granted the kindness they show
Disclose your love for them and make sure they know.
So give back these qualities and then in the end

...........you'll know the blessing of a really

TRUE FRIEND

VISIT OF CHARITY

Small, fair and bright as a band-boy's button
The Girl Guide ascends the Rest Home steps,
Shifting the potted plant from hand to hand.

She wears a red coat and blue velour hat
And has come with a yellow chrysanthemum,
Drooping through lack of water.

Setting down the plant she removes her mittens
Before opening the thin glass door.
The building is cold; like a block of ice.

"I have come to see an old lady"
She tells the uniformed nurse,
"I am a Girl Guide and I need another badge.
Any old lady will do."

THE READER

Jamie had been told to take a book to the "Read-Write-Centre" - any book, Gran had said. Which was all the same to him because even though he was twelve years old he had never learned to read; although he had spent hours in Combridges and W.H. Smiths looking along the rows of brightly coloured paperbacks.

"All you have to do, Jamie," Gran had said, "is to go along to the Church Hall in Bonchurch Road tomorrow morning. I've paid for you to join the Read-Write-Centre. They'll have you reading in no time."

Jamie had looked at Gran with surprise. She was the only person who really cared anything about him, but he hadn't thought even she knew how desperately he wanted to learn to read.

"I saw it advertised in the Newsagent's window," Gran went on. "It's being run by a retired teacher during the school holidays. All you have to do is be there sharp at ten tomorrow morning. Take a book with you - any book will do. They guarantee to have you reading by the end of your first lesson."

This had excited but dismayed him at the same time, for his parents weren't readers either. He reckoned there wouldn't be a book to be found in his sleazy council flat - unless you counted the tabloid newspaper Dad liked with the page three ladies, but he didn't think the Read-Write-Centre would much care for that.

Now "tomorrow morning" had arrived and the bent hand on the cracked china wall-clock pointed to quarter to ten. He had searched everywhere he could think of in the flat, even under his bed where he'd found a half-eaten chocolate biscuit, green with age and a well-sucked "gob-stopper" still sticky and covered in fluff. His father had popped out to the betting shop and his mother next door to Mrs Turner's, leaving the dirty breakfast dishes in the sink. Usually he rinsed and drained them for her, to keep on the "right side" and

avoid getting a clip around the ear. But today the dishes were forgotten because of the more important issue at hand.

Suddenly Jamie made up his mind. Grabbing his skimpy blazer from the back of the kitchen door, he slammed out of the flat, across the communal hall with its graffiti walls and through the depressing main entrance. He had never stolen anything in his life - but now the time had come for drastic action. In no time he was up in the High Street where all the bright shops were, making his way towards the lovely exciting atmosphere of his local bookshop. Once inside he began looking discreetly along the familiar colourful shelves where the garish paperbacks stood like rows of Roman sentinels. There were so many of them and all equally inviting.

But before long he had the uncomfortable feeling he was being watched by the chinless mousy-haired assistant with the bifocals. He wondered if she recognised him from his numerous visits to the shop in the past, although he'd never had enough money to buy anything. Hunching up his shoulders and keeping his head well down he moved to the other side of the shop. This was a section he'd not bothered with before because it seemed less interesting.

Here the books were quite drab. No skulls and crossbones or daggers dripping with blood adorned their jackets. Jamie screwed up his nose in distaste. He was just wasting precious time here - none of these books looked suitable for the Read-Write class. Then suddenly one particular volume caught his eye. It stood out from all the rest with its shiny red and yellow jacket. Red had always been his very favourite colour. Jamie glanced around. There was no-one looking. He took the book from the shelf and ran a grubby hand over its smooth and slippery surface, even holding it to his nose for a moment, sniffing the delicious tangy aroma of its cover. He thought of all the knowledge the book might

contain. Things he might be able to learn about if they could teach him to read at the Read-Write-Centre.

But also he thought about Gran. She wouldn't want him to steal. "Stealing is breaking the eighth commandment," he'd heard her once say. Yet if he hadn't got a book to take to the Centre, it would be no use him going - and then he would be letting Gran down. The temptation was too much. Still keeping his head down, he swiveled his eyes from side to side, taking in the length of the shop in both directions. There was no sign of old "bifocals". He paused for just a moment. Then quickly, and with a sleight of hand an experienced kleptomaniac would have been proud of, Jamie deftly filched the book away into his inside blazer pocket, next to his heart.

He reached the Church Hall just after ten o'clock and hurriedly gave his name to a studious looking lady sitting at a small table just inside the arched entrance. She ticked his name off a list and directed him to the lecture room. It was similar to a school room with a blackboard at the far end, but instead of squat desks, like at his old school - which he'd seldom attended because of the many domestic problems of his parents - there were three long trestle tables, reminding him of the one Dad had borrowed last year when Mum had nagged him into decorating their front room. The tables were set up across the width of the room and were already occupied by potential students.

An elderly lady with short springy hair came forward drawing him into the room. "Come on now, we are just about to begin. Take a seat." She indicated the table nearest him, and with much shuffling of feet two lads, older than himself, pushed along making a space for him. Gratefully he sat down, conscious of curious eyes upon him.

"Now I hope you have all brought a book," said the teacher running a kindly eye over them all whilst they settled back into their seats. "It is my intention to have

you all reading at least one paragraph of your chosen book before you leave here today." She smiled around the class benevolently.

Jamie's heart leapt in anticipation.

"Please place your books on the table before you," she instructed.

Jamie did so, proudly. He felt his book with its red and yellow cover was the shiniest, newest and most interesting one of all. Slowly the teacher walked along behind the three rows of students, leaning over each one in turn, endeavouring to see what each person had brought. Now she was behind Jamie.

"Right my dear, let me see......open your book."

Jamie did as he was bid; turning back its glossy cover so that the title page was exposed. He ran his finger over the bold black print, longing to be able to make sense of the tantalising, incomprehensible words.

Like a soft white bird, one of the teacher's hands flew to her mouth, suppressing a gasp. For a moment time stood still and one could have heard a pin drop. Jamie's book was entitled "Tales of My Fatherland" and apart from a few English footnotes, it was written entirely in German.

Spare a Prayer for the Animals

SPARE A PRAYER FOR THE ANIMALS

Spare a prayer for the animals
Remember the pleasure they bring.
The feel of a cat when it purrs on your lap
Is a soothing and comforting thing.

Spare a prayer for the animals
The spaniel with trusting brown eyes
That follow you around, wherever you go
With a love that it cannot disguise.

Look at the horse, so beautifully made
A creature of strength and delight.
Yet so sensitive that the smallest of things
Can instantly put him to flight.

Remember that God made the animals
And left them in our tender care.
So spare a prayer for the animals
Keep them safe in the world we all share.

LITTLE TORTY

Written for my friends Brenda & Ron when they lost their little tortoise friend who had lived with them for many years.

Our little tortoise died today
We are so very sad.
He'd been with us for many years
And was a lovely lad!

Before we owned him, he'd been dropped
And had a dodgy shell,
But with our tender loving care
He soon got fit and well

His favourite food was strawberries
He liked tomatoes too
But if we lacked these tasty treats -
Then dandelions would do.

We're sorry little Torty,
We'll miss your funny face
We think your age was thirty years
But only by God's grace.

So now we're hoping you have gone
Where all good tortoises go
To a heaven full of juicy snacks
Where strawberries always grow.

EASTER DONKEY

I found a little donkey
He'd only just been born.
He lay beside his mother
So soft and sweet and warm.

Soon he tried to struggle up
On legs so long and thin
But couldn't get the hang of it
So fell back down again.

And by the look of puzzlement
Upon his worried face
T'was clear he thought this great big world
A complicated place.

And then I noticed something else
……..it was the "tell-tale" sign.
It stretched along his curly coat
And made him…..so divine.

I pray he'll meet with kindness
When people realise that
He wears the cross of our dear Lord
Upon his shaggy back.

MY BIRD

My bird I put inside a golden cage
And kept him in the sunny window bay
So that he had the brightness of the day.
And in the evening when the shade
Sent the wild bird to its nest
I covered over my bird for its rest.

But somehow, after I had gone to bed
I couldn't get the thought out of my head
What life had he shut in that tiny space
Looking out beyond the curtain lace?
What joy had wings that couldn't open wide
And songs that wouldn't reach the trees outside?

So in the morning when the sun had risen
I went to let my bird out of his prison
But oh! Too late, for his small heart had broken
His gentle soul had flown from cage unopen
So now when I hear birdsong from above
I like to think he's free......within God's love.

MY LITTLE ELEPHANT

I'd like a little elephant
With skin of pearly grey.
I'd wash him down with Fairy Snow
And scrub his ears each day.

I'd give his feet a manicure.
I'd use my best nail file
And when I'd got him spic and span
I'd let him rest awhile.

Then off we'd go to Sainsbury's
He'd just squeeze through the door.
He'd push the trolley with his trunk
.......it's not against the law.

And when we'd got the shopping done
I'd take him home for tea.
I don't know what he'd want to eat
......I hope the same as me.

Then when it reached his time for bed
I'd put his "jim jams" on
And find a pillow large enough
To rest his head upon.

But just before he went to sleep
I hope he'd say a prayer
Asking God to safely keep
Elephants.....everywhere.

MY OLD TOM CAT

What's happened to my old Tom cat
.....the one that was a stray?
The one I took such pity on
I let him in to stay.

The seat's still warm where last he sat
But there's no sign of him.
He's usually waiting here for me
As soon as I get in.

He likes to "pussy foot" around
And rules the house by day
But always when he hears my voice
He purrs and comes to play.

I wonder where he's got to?
He must be somewhere near.
It's funny how an old Tom cat
Becomes so very dear.

But wait.....was that a feint meow
From somewhere 'neath the stair?
I'm sure if I go take a look
I'll find him hiding there.

Yes.....it is my old Tom cat
With a big surprise for me.
Three fluffy kittens nestle there
My old Tom cat's a She.

CATS DON'T CARE

Cats can sleep just anywhere
In a window, on a chair
Along a small and narrow ledge
On the very table edge.
Anywhere......they don't care.

Cats can sleep just any place
On a box or in a case
Dreaming in the noonday sun
Snoozing when the day is done.
Any time......these feline

Cats can sleep through anything
Thunder storms and doorbells ring
Even when the baby cries
Cats can always close their eyes.
Anywhere......they don't care.

"SCATS"

Some people say "Scats" when talking to cats
And don't like the way they behave
But I think they're great - so serene and sedate
And always incredibly brave.
They do have their faults - well, we all have our warts
But cats have only a few.
They quite like to play - but must have their way.
You won't win whatever you do.
Their claws will go in and puncture your skin.
Your tights will end up with a run.
But they're always sublime, these furry feline
And love you to tickle their tum.
They'll purr with delight when you come into sight
Then walk aloofly away.
But if you live alone - get a cat in your home
You'll have love and a laugh every day.

THE BUTTERFLY

To my friend Irene who, on seeing a white butterfly hovering over her late husband's pillow, took it as a sign of his presence in the home and has never felt lonely since.

That day I felt so sad and low
I needed just to cry.
My loved one seemed so far away
Why had God let him die?

I went into our bedroom
And stood beside our bed
When suddenly a butterfly
Fluttered o'er my head.

It settled on the pillow where
I rested every night
That fragile, shimmering butterfly
Was such a lovely sight.

But I didn't understand just how
In December……winter time,
A butterfly could still exist
Unless it was a sign!

Then something made me turn around
I really don't know why
But I felt a loving presence
Was standing there, close by.

I looked back for the butterfly
Though by then, it had gone
Yet this I know, I'll ne'er forget
How brightly it had shone.

I never found that butterfly
Although I searched my home
But since the day I saw it,
I've never felt alone.

SYDNEY THE SNAIL

Poor Sydney the snail was looking quite pale,
His shell lacked the lustre of youth.
He'd lived in his house for such a long time
- he needed to find a new roof.

He'd seen other snails with bright shiny shells
- he'd like to get one for himself
And in his tiny mind, if he could just find
A new shell, t'would be good for his health.

But wherever he went, there were no shells to rent,
They all seemed to have snails inside.
No matter how hard he banged on their doors
It was clear they were all occupied.

So he slithered around on the "rainy" wet ground
With his little snail mind in a muddle,
Then feeling unwell, he fell back in his shell
And promptly rolled into a puddle.

But when he came to, the skies had turned blue
And the puddle had washed his shell brightly.
It sparkled and shone and looked good as new
And Sydney himself, felt quite sprightly.

This just goes to show that when you feel low
And all of your plans seem to fail
There's someone "up there" who really does care
Yes - even for Sydney the snail.

THE FUNNY GIRAFFE

Some people may think
that God's made a gaffe
by creating for us
the funny giraffe.

With its neck so long
and its legs like sticks
and its huge rough tongue
of a thousand "licks".

But it gathers its food
from the tops of the trees
so its long long neck
can reach up with ease.

And its comical face
has such beautiful eyes
with the loveliest lashes
ever devised.

And another good thing
- which is rather sweet -
It's a strict vegetarian
never eats meat.

So at the end of the day
I think you'll applaud,
that the funny giraffe
is much blessed by the Lord.

A CUDDLE FOR CODGER

This was written when I worked as a kennel-maid for a vets in Great Yarmouth. The kennels were beside a river and had been made from old stables. They weren't all that comfortable, but the dogs and cats (who had separate living quarters upstairs, thank goodness) were all loved and well cared for, and like Codger they were given plenty of cuddles.

He was an old dog, long past his prime, and his master was an old rag and bone man. They often passed the entrance of the kennels where I worked, on Great Yarmouth Bridge, the man pushing his barrow of rags and oddities and the old dog trotting faithfully behind. But one day the rag and bone man turned his barrow in under the archway and beckoned me to him.

"It's like this," he began, "I've got to go into hospital for a fortnight. Could you board the old Codger for me?"

I looked down at the black, rough-coated mongrel - the first time I'd seen him up close. It was love at first sight! Codger came into the kennels the same day as his master went into hospital and I tried to make him as comfortable as possible. The kennels had been converted from stables - divided into pens by mesh wire. Not the most up-to-date accommodation, but clean and roomy, with plenty of sweet-smelling straw for bedding.

However, Codger, who was used to trotting freely with his master, didn't settle in at all well. He whined a great deal and refused the food I offered. It was August week too - when I was extra busy and unable to give him individual attention. Apart from fresh clients to see, there were runs to scrub down, food to prepare and other animals to attend. Putting it mildly, I was rushed off my feet.

By the end of the week, Codger was in a bad way. It was on the Friday and I was dishing up the evening feed

that the most heart-rending howl came from his pen. On investigating, I was horrified. He had climbed up the wire mesh on the door and was clinging on with his claws, his whole body stiff and taut as a board. Codger was having a fit. I managed to get him down and sat on the straw bed with him in my arms.

I rocked him to and fro like a baby, talking gently to him all the time. Soon his body relaxed and then I gave him a really good cuddle.

After this he improved rapidly. He began eating his food and seemed to adapt himself to his new surroundings. It was as if this was a crisis in his life and he'd decided to get over it. But there was still a sadness in his eyes.

Then came the wonderful day when the old rag and bone man came home from hospital and claimed him. Codger was frantic with delight and licked the old man's face all over.

"I nearly 'ad it Miss y'know," the rag and bone man said, unashamedly wiping a tear from his eye with the back of a gnarled hand. "That first Friday night I 'ad a crisis but I knew I 'ad to hang on for old Codger's sake."

I watched them walk away together, as happy as sandboys. I didn't tell the old man that Codger had had a crisis too.

Many times afterwards the rag and bone man and his faithful companion went past the archway of the kennels. They always paused, looking in my direction. Old Codger would wag his tail warily... from a distance. But he would never allow himself to be enticed any nearer. That was a shame... for I would have loved to have given him another really good cuddle!

Remembering

REMEMBER I'M STILL ME

Former carer Margaret Randall from Brighton looked after her husband John for 15 years until his death. Like many carers, Margaret found that it helped to write down her feelings - especially when things went wrong! John suffered from Parkinson's disease and Margaret managed to look after him at home - with the help of professional carers. Margaret says that writing poems helped her through the stressful times. "Remember I'm Still Me" was written for John.

Extract from Yours Magazine

I know I'm growing shaky
My tremors I can't hide
But please remember when we meet
That I'm still ME inside.

My words may not come easily
For you to understand
But can't you see, I really want
To smile and shake your hand.

Don't leave me in a corner
Forgetting that I'm there.
I'm part of life the same as you
And need your loving care.

Fate has dealt this sorry blow
It cannot be denied
But remember when you look at me
That I'm still ME inside.

PLEASE SAY MY NAME

"Please Say My Name" was written by Margaret for a friend whose husband suffered from Alzheimer's disease.

Extract from Yours Magazine

You used to know me once, dear,
You used to call my name.
We were so close together,
Before your illness came.

We shared our tears and laughter,
Our rapport was so good.
I only had to catch your eye
And you always understood.

But now you don't remember,
I see that vacant gaze,
To you I'm just a stranger,
Who helps you through your days.

I try not to let it hurt me,
And yet of course it does,
I only hope you understand,
The measure of my love.

Sometimes I sense the "old you",
A smile - a laugh - a touch.
If only you could say my name,
Yes - that would mean so much.

LOSS

Written with loving thoughts for my dear friends Doreen and Pete who lost their most precious son Mark in 1996

When you lose a loved one
It may be hard to pray
You wonder why a loving God
Has taken him away.

You cry a million, million tears
Until your eyes are dry
And ask yourself a thousand times
WHY......WHY......WHY?

You walk into a familiar room
And see his vacant chair
You wish you could put back the clock
And see him sitting there.

Someone turns the radio on
It plays his favourite song
Time stretches out before you
Each day so sad......so long.

You wonder how you'll manage
With all this pain inside.
You tend to draw within yourself
And from the world to hide.

But then one day you'll notice
The glimmer of the sun
A patch of golden daffodils
Spring has just begun.

There'll be a lightening of your step
......an easing of the pain
You'll thank God for a lovely day
And start living life again.

Happy Thoughts

CONTEMPLATE A MIRACLE

Contemplate a miracle
You'll find that one will come
Like snowdrops during wintertime
And butterflies in sun.

Take a poignant memory
That's locked within your heart
Fetch it out and reminisce
... then make another start.

Forget those pains and grievances
And start the day anew
Looking only for the good
... and good will come to you.

Remember everyone has pain
So keep your mind alert
And always be there ready
To help another's hurt.

Don't grow old and cold within
Step out into the sun.
Contemplate a miracle
Then one is sure to come.

A SPECIAL PLACE

You've got a "special" place in life
A "special" role to play.
No one else can take that place
Or live your "special" way.

You may not think you matter much
In this great big world we share
But God has blessed you through and through
And counted every hair.

He has a "special" plan for you
Where e'er you are today
There is a duty to perform
In your own "special" way.

It might be just a few kind words
To someone who's lost hope
... or sharing someone's burden
And helping them to cope.

There is a "special" thread to weave
So do the best you can
Completing life's rich tapestry
According to God's plan.

M. B 26-8-2012

GOLDEN DREAM

Keep a golden dream
Deep within your heart
Never lose the sight of it
Or let that dream depart

INSTANT SUN

When you see a glimpse of sun
Don't linger in the shade
But catch it fast in your mind's eye
So it will never fade.

Then when the cold dark winter comes
And you're feeling low and glum
Let that sparkling memory
Provide your instant sun.

IT'S THE LITTLE THINGS THAT MATTER

It's the little things that matter
... that make the world go round
It's not the great deeds planned in prayer
That are the most profound.

It's knowing when to praise awhile
... to take the time to cheer
Someone who is feeling low
Or needs to shed a tear.

Big things sometimes "solve themselves"
... for people "rise above".
It's the little things where we can help
... that need our gentle love.

It's good sometimes to think folk see
The kind things that we do,
But more important are those deeds
Of kindness... not in view.

So be alert to little things
Where we can give our love
And know our heavenly Father
Is watching from above.

MY PLACE

You've put me in this "place" Lord
I didn't choose it for myself
I would have picked an easier path
Less hassle and more wealth

But now that I am here Lord
According to your grace
I'll try to make my piece of earth
A kinder, happier place.

Family and Friends

TO MY DAUGHTER

My friend Floss wanted to say a big "Thank you" to her daughter in words of poetry.

That day you came into my life
The whole world changed for me.
I knew the love between us two
Would always, always be.

You were my very special gift
A jewel of priceless worth
I think the good Lord up above
Sent you, for me on earth.

But now the years are going by
I just want you to know
How wonderful I think you are
For Sue… I love you so.

You're always there to help me
When things are going wrong
You just reach out and put things right
So I can carry on.

You're more than just my daughter
You are my best friend too
You are my strength, my steadfast rock
I so depend on you.

So thank you Sue, for everything
Your kindness and your care
There's nothing greater than this bond
Of love that we two share.

MY GRANDMOTHER'S HOUSE

I'll always remember my grandmother's house
- the comfort and love I found there,
As I sat with the glow of the fire on my face,
Curled up in her old Windsor chair.

I remember the clink of her best china cups
As she reached them down from the shelf,
Setting them out on saucers that matched
- one for me... and one for herself.

T'was my turn to toast the muffins for tea
- the task that I liked most of all.
Spreading the butter in thick golden blobs
Careful... in case some should fall.

The sound of the kettle aboil on the hob
Made beautiful music to me
And watching dear gran as she warmed up the pot,
Ready for "mashing" the tea.

There's now nothing left of grandmother's house
And granny - she died years ago
But I pray if she's watching from Heaven above
She'll realise... that I loved her so.

A MEMORY OF HOME

Granny Garner measured the width of the mantelpiece between her thumb and forefinger. It was narrow, but she was sure the alabaster clock would have stood safely on it, even if it might have overlapped a bit. Still, she supposed Esther was right. What sense was there in bringing the old clock when there was already a perfectly good electric one in her room? As there was in every room of her daughter's ultra-modern house.

"Mother," Esther called up the stairs, "are you coming down for tea? It's on the table."

Gran tidied her silver hair and fastened her brooch more securely at the neck of her shawl. Her late husband, Edward, had given her the cameo brooch as a birthday present and she didn't want to lose it. It was a pity, she thought, as she started down the curved staircase, that Esther hadn't inherited a little of her father's tenderness and understanding. Over the past few months especially, her daughter had grown more and more cold and unfeeling... just like the new house.

Granny Garner paused, reprimanding herself. After all, it was generous of Esther and Tom to have given her a home after her cottage had been pulled down to make room for the new road. Of course, there had been the compensation from the council which she had handed straight over to Tom; but they'd used part of it on having an extra bathroom built next to her room for her own personal use. So she mustn't go finding fault. Gran held the curving handrail as she descended. How she hated these modern stairs. Nothing but slats of wood with wide spaces between so that she could see the polished floor below. The whole journey from the top of the stairs, across the slippery hall to the modern kitchen, was a nightmare to her.

"Come on, Mother - I've already poured your tea." Esther slid the thick earthenware cup and saucer over

the formica tabletop. "It's almost cold," she said, not bothering to disguise the irritation in her voice.

"I'm sorry dear," Gran apologised, thinking of the bone china and snow white tablecloths she'd always used in her own comfortable kitchen in the cottage.

"We've been waiting ages," Miranda, her six-year-old granddaughter, said accusingly. "I wanted to start my egg but Mummy wouldn't let me..."

"Oh dear, I am in everyone's bad books," Gran chuckled, trying to make light of it.

"Well, I do like people to be punctual for meals," Esther said without humour.

Gran sat down and sipped her tea.

"We're having visitors tonight Gran," Miranda confided, primly. "Mummy's going to let me stay up if I'm a good girl. Aren't you, Mummy?"

"We'll see," Esther replied, her manner softening a little as she cut off the top of Miranda's egg. "The Grahams are coming Mother. You've met them, haven't you?"

Gran nodded. She had met the Grahams - and hadn't liked them. She'd found them pretentious and boring and full of themselves. She knew they regarded her as old-fashioned and dull.

"What about wearing your oatmeal dress with the pretty collar when they come?" Esther suggested. "That shawl does rather make you look like Whistler's Mother."

Gran's hand moved up to the cameo brooch and traced its pattern with shaking fingers. Did Esther know how cruel she was being?

"I... I might stay in my room tonight," she said, "I've got some mending to do... and there's some good music on the radio."

"Oh, I don't want you to feel you're not welcome Mother," Esther protested, but Gran detected a note of relief in her voice.

Gran was glad to get back into her room, although it

still remained unfriendly and cold in spite of her efforts to make it homely. She had wanted to bring her bow-fronted chest of drawers and her mahogany wardrobe. But Esther had put her foot down. "That's silly, Mother," she'd said, "when there's a lovely built-in wall cupboard and dressing table. You won't need any of your furniture. Anyway, we'd never get that great wardrobe of yours up our stairs."

Sadly, Gran had agreed and it was arranged that Tom would sell up most of her belongings. But they had let her bring her winged chair. Funnily enough, it had been Tom who'd decided on this.

"Poor old girl," she'd heard him say one evening when she was quietly drying the supper dishes in the kitchen. He and Esther had been sitting at the other side of the alcove finishing their coffee and hadn't realised she was still there. "She needs to have her own comfortable chair. After all it'll be in her room, so it won't clash with our modern stuff!"

"I suppose not," Esther had replied reluctantly. "But now we've got this house at last, we don't want it cluttered up with museum pieces. I hope everything is going to work out all right, Tom," she added doubtfully.

"Well, we can't leave the old girl with nowhere to go... and you must admit, she's a bit past coping for herself now. Anyway, she's got her name down on the list for the Old Age Pensioners Home, so until then we'll have to manage."

It was a bit of a shock to learn that your nearest and dearest thought you were "past it" and were only waiting for the time when they could pack you safely away in a home...

"Of course, there was the compensation money," Esther had gone on, her voice brightening a little. "It came in very handy, and it's useful having another bathroom in the house."

Now, Gran wondered if she's dreamed their conversation that evening. Surely Esther couldn't have

been so mercenary. But she had to admit her daughter had grown farther and farther away from her lately, until it was difficult to believe they were mother and daughter any more.

With a sigh, Gran sank down into her old armchair. It's high back and winged sides enveloped her small body, giving her warmth and comfort. One thing was certain, she thought with relief, she wouldn't be meeting the Grahams tonight, for she had made up her mind that from now on, she would stay in her room when Esther had visitors. That way she would be less of a nuisance to them all. Even Miranda, her granddaughter, was a disappointment with her prim manner and wheedling ways. So unlike Esther at that age, warm and lovable and full of interesting chatter. Why had she grown into a disagreeable woman?

It was then she had the idea. She would show them she wasn't "past it". Tomorrow was Saturday and Esther would be going shopping in the morning. It would be a good opportunity for her to creep out of the house and back to Tavistock Lane. Her cottage might not be there anymore, but she would see all the old familiar roads and shops and maybe meet someone she knew. It would be quite an adventure for her... and she needed desperately to see her old surroundings again.

Next morning dawned dry and sunny. From her window Gran watched Esther and Miranda walking down the front path. When they reached the end of the road she slid open the door of the wall cupboard, put on her coat and pulled on her soft, blue velvet hat, tucking stray tendrils of hair into place. She hated to recall how old the hat was - but it had been Edward's favourite. She remembered him saying that it exactly matched the blue of her eyes. Now, checking her appearance in the mirror, she couldn't help thinking how both the hat and her eyes had faded since those days. With her handbag clutched beneath her arm she descended the dreaded stairs, surprised that they didn't hold the usual fear for

her... probably because the anticipation of her journey was uppermost in her mind.

As she passed the houses on the new estate on her way to the bus stop, she noticed how ugly and alike they all were. It was as if robots lived in them, not real living and breathing people! The bus was already there when she arrived at the stop and she got on, thankful it would soon be carrying her back to her old "haunts". It was exactly as she remembered it. Violet Road where Mrs Pearcey lived, Lovedale Crescent with its semicircle of trees where she'd pushed Esther as a baby in a pram, the little row of shops and Bennets the grocers, now boarded up, where she had handed in her weekly order. But when she walked around the corner towards Tavistock Lane where her cottage had stood, her knees trembled and a lump came to her throat. There was nothing left but an empty piece of land, flattened by bulldozers. Even the garden had been demolished. Not a sign of a rose tree or the sweet smelling stocks that had been her pride and joy.

For a few minutes she stood there with a great sense of loss, almost wishing that she hadn't come. Then, gathering herself together, she turned and walked back. But as she retraced her footsteps past the shops - she saw the alabaster clock. It was in the front of the second-hand shop window. She drew nearer, bending down a little and peering intently through her glasses. Was it really her clock? Yes... there was the small stain on the delicate alabaster made by Edward's pipe, which he'd always kept in a rack on the mantelpiece beside it.

Gathering courage, she pushed open the shop door. A youngish man came through the plastic strip curtain from the back. "What can I do for you?" he asked.

She wanted to tell him that it was her clock in the window - her's and Edward's - but he didn't look the type of person who would understand.

"That... that clock!" she said at last. "What are you asking for it?"

"Three pounds," the young man answered, taking out a cigarette and lighting it.

Gran's heart sank. Three pounds! Such a lot of money to pay to get one's own property back - and besides she knew she didn't have that much on her. Feverishly, she hunted in her purse. "I... I couldn't possibly pay that much," she said lamely.

The young man looked at her shrewdly. "Tell you what Mrs... you can have it for two pounds fifty, not a penny less," he said, making a great play of his generosity.

Granny Garner hesitated. She was in a dilemma. Two pounds fifty was all the money she had. If she bought the clock she would have to walk home for she hadn't a penny piece more - and she was too proud to ask the man to make the price any less. She got out two pound coins and a fifty pence piece from her purse and handed them over. Edward would have wanted her to have the clock. The young man wrapped it clumsily in a sheet of brown paper.

How she managed to get home she didn't know. The clock was much heavier than she'd remembered. She opened the front gate gently and crept up the path, hoping Esther wouldn't see her, although it was clear she and Miranda were home, for their coats were hanging in the hall. Gran got up to her room and sank thankfully down into her winged chair, too tired even to remove her hat and coat. The paper had come loose from the clock as she sat with it in her aching arms, staring down at it fondly.

She was fast asleep when Esther stole into her room with a cup of tea. She had seen her mother come in and been appalled by the pathetic way the old lady had clutched the clock to her. Putting the tea down on the side table, Esther bent gently over the winged chair. All at once she realised what the clock meant to her mother. It was part of the past not just an old-fashioned clock but a link with Father - with the old home and

even her own happy childhood. She suddenly felt very ashamed.

Esther didn't attempt to take the clock from her mother's lap for she looked so content with it resting there. But she vowed in her heart to make it all up to the old lady; and leaning down she started her new resolution there and then - by dropping a loving kiss on her mother's forehead.

MOTHERS ARE PRECIOUS

Mothers are precious so when you are young
Take care with the words that trip off your tongue.
Don't be too hasty and sharp with replies
Lest you bring the tears to your mother's eyes.
Remember she loves you through good times and bad.
Think of those moments when you made her sad.
The young can be selfish, though they don't mean to be
But we all in our youth think only of "me".
So next time you're feeling bad-tempered and vexed
Just hold fast your tongue and dwell on this text.
Mothers are precious when all's said and done
So love and respect her......you only get one.

MY MOTHER'S FACE

I tried to paint a picture
Of my mother's face
But no way could I capture
Her beauty or her grace.
It seemed to me the canvas
Lay taut beneath my touch
And wouldn't flex that gentle smile
That I had loved so much.
I chose a heavenly colour
To depict her eyes of blue
But couldn't catch the love light
Always shining through.
So then I paused and thought awhile
At what a fool I'd been
For the beauty of my mother
Was her spirit deep within
But you cannot paint a spirit
The spirit is divine
Nor can you paint the sweetest soul
Of a mother such as mine.

QUEEN OF THE ROAD

"Come on Jessie... come in with me." Mog's scrawny hand pulled at her arm. "It's a good place... you'll see, and we'll get a lovely Christmas dinner for free."

But Jessie wouldn't budge. She didn't like to look of the grey stone Hostel, no matter how many "WELCOME" posters were stuck in the windows and pinned on the huge front door. The more Mog clawed at her arm the firmer Jessie planted her feet in their scabby Wellingtons on the muddy verge outside.

"You go in if you must; get yerself a free dinner with all the trimmings but I ain't setting foot in there."

Mog sniffed. She already had the beginning of a cold and now snow had started to fall.

"Besides, you don't know what kind of people you'll meet", Jessie went on. "They'll probably pinch your stuff or swear like troopers... you won't like that Mog, not with your Methodist upbringing."

But as the two friends stood arguing, Jessie's resolve almost wavered as the tantalizing savoury smells drifted up from the gratings of the Hostel's basement kitchen.

"Come on Jess," Mog had one more try, "think of all that turkey and plum pud... on proper china plates too - it'll do us both the world of good - besides I'll freeze to death if I don't get in the warm soon."

Jessie snorted, pushing temptation away. "Thought you liked our kind of life; thought you prided yerself on being a 'Queen of the Road' she challenged scornfully.

Mog's chin trembled. "So I do," she protested, pulling her moth-eaten coat moretightly around her skinny frame... "but I'm going in anyway. Lummy, it's only for one measly Christmas dinner."

Jessie watched her stumble up the steps to the Hostel door, a strange scarecrow of a figure in the old fur coat she'd bought at a jumble for a few pence when they'd first met. Mog had worn it ever since; and the nick-name that went so fittingly with it. On the top step she turned,

and gave a half-hearted wave before disappearing inside. Jessie shrugged. She knew once the warmth seeped into Mog's bones, she'd never come out on the Road again. She'd seen the signs recently on Mog's pinched face. It was sad, but she wasn't going to worry about it even though they'd been mates for a long time now. You have to be tough to survive the travelling life... and Mog wasn't. She'd had quite a genteel upbringing and was ten years older than Jessie; and every year counted against you 'on the road'. Jessie stopped walking and stamped her frozen feet back to life. The Christmas afternoon was slipping into darkness already and the temperature dropping. She'd better get back to the squat... at least the old derelict house she and Mog had found was a good shelter, built of bricks and mortar, with a proper fireplace; not just a cardboard box like some poor souls had to endure.

As she was passing along the backs of the big sea front hotels that always seemed to do a good trade at Christmas, a man in a chef's white jacket came out. Jessie thought he was going to tell her off, although she wasn't scrounging, but he turned back into the premises, only to re-appear carrying something wrapped in silver foil.

"Here you are Mrs," he came towards her, thrusting the parcel into her hands. Then stooping, he dropped a can of Guinness into the roomy pocket of her coat. "Don't see why you shouldn't have some of the spoils... probably appreciate it more than some of those 'stuffed shirts' in there." He jerked his head back towards the hotel.

Jessie stood, open mouthed in amazement; then hastily stuffed the parcel into the bosom of her coat where it lay warm and comforting against her breast, she quickened her pace lest he should have second thoughts, and hurried 'home' as fast as her legs and the slippery pavements allowed.

Back in the squat she opened the parcel. It contained

a feast of succulent mouth-watering turkey. She was tempted to eat the lot there and then... but instead chewed on a plump drumstick whilst putting a match to the remainder of the wood she and Mog had left in the broken grate earlier that day. As the flames darted and crackled, she dragged the old striped mattress nearer the fire and plumped herself down. Then, remembering the Guinness she pulled it from her pocket, removed the ring-pull and took a good long swig. Mog wouldn't have approved... but all the same she wished she was with her now. It was always good to have company at Christmas. Still, Mog would be better off where she was. Soon the warmth from the fire and the Guinness had their effect... and she slumped back on the dingy mattress in a peaceful sleep.

It was late evening when she awoke and the snow had stopped. For a moment she'd forgotten what day it was until her eyes fell on the silver parcel of goodies. Of course, there was still a little bit more of Christmas to celebrate. Now feeling ravenously hungry she unwrapped the turkey, spreading it out on the foil and automatically dividing it into two portions... then with a pang, realised what she was doing. What a fool... who did she think she was going to share it with?

As if in answer to her thoughts, a sound came from outside. Her heart leapt. Could it be Mog back again? Jessie opened the rickety back door a crack and peered out. It wasn't Mog but a little brown dog snuffling about, its nose encrusted with snow. He cowered when he first saw her, but encouraged by a morsel of turkey... (well why not, she had plenty), she was able to entice him inside. Soon the turkey was eaten and the mongrel stretched out beside her with his head on her lap in front of the rekindled fire. She was really chuffed with his company. Maybe it would be a good idea to keep him. He'd be able to walk miles without moaning about blisters, and follow her anywhere she wanted to go... John O'Groats if need be.

Lost in happy reverie Jessie's head began to droop... pictures of green fields and pastures new formed in her dreaming mind until her own loud snores awoke her with a start... and it was Boxing Day morning. The fire was out... and the little dog gone. He must have squeezed past the loose slats in the back door.

"Of all the ungrateful beggars." Jessie muttered, but deep in her heart she understood. The little dog, like her, valued his own independence.

Stretching up her arms in a yawn, Jessie contemplated her Christmas. On the whole it hadn't been too bad. She'd had plenty to eat, a warm place to sleep and company, thanks to the little dog - but now her dreams had given her itchy feet again.

She looked around the room. It had been a good squat during the few months she and Mog had shared it - but now Mog had gone there was no reason to stay. Besides, she rather fancied Kent; such pretty countryside, especially at hop-picking time. She got up and began gathering her meagre bits and pieces together. Outside the grubby window she was pleased to see the snow had almost cleared. Reason told her she should wait for the better weather - but it was such a bright encouraging day, and now that she'd decided to move on she could hardly wait to get going. If she worked her way around the coastline she could rest-up at all the little seaside towns along the way until she got to Dover... Yes, that's what she'd do. Determinedly she bent and pulled on the scabby wellingtons she'd discarded the night before... she'd make her way to Dover, then go inland a bit... and arrive in plenty of time for the hop-picking season.

AUNT HANNAH'S HATS

This is written in memory of my dear Aunt Nan who really loved hats. In her day no self-respecting woman would be without one and my aunt had several, mostly of her own creation. Her bedroom was like an Aladdin's cave adorned with snippets of tulles and satins and velvet ribbons waiting to adorn one of her favourite old hats to make it look even more beautiful. As a child I thought how lovely it would be to give auntie her own hat shop - but it wasn't to be. However, now, with a little poetic license, maybe it's come true.

When I was a child it wasn't the thing for ladies to work for a living. Yet no kitchen maid worked as hard as my Aunt Hannah did on her hats. Her bedroom was a delight of snippets of satin and shimmers of silk. It was heaven to poke around in the corners and come across some unexpected treasure... a pink velvet rose made especially for a friend, or a handful of tulle awaiting creation.

Eventually our family hit upon hard times. Money was scarce and something had to be done. Aunt Hannah came to the rescue. She had seen a little lock-up shop, no larger than a doll's house, in the High Street, and against the advice of the family rented it for a few shillings a week.

You can imagine how proud I was when she asked me to draw and paint a sign for her to hang on the shop door reading A Hannah Hat for a Happy Face. As if by some magic the message on the sign really seemed to work. Whether it was the hats themselves, or my aunt's cheerful philosophy, I'll never know - but harassed faces came into the shop and went out again wreathed in smiles beneath my Aunt's beautiful handiwork. Even Mrs Broadblow, a well-known 'grump' in the community, had a softer light in her eyes. I don't think anyone had ever noticed they were quite such a nice shade of blue before

they looked out from beneath a Hannah creation of turquoise velvet.

Soon Hannah's Hats became quite a cult in our small town. People came from far and wide to buy for special occasions. Easter Bonnets in eggshell blue with flowing ribbons went like hot cakes, and my Aunt's Festival Hats, golden straw and adorned with succulent imitation fruit, were the talk of the town. Many of the ladies of our parish were seen wearing them to church on Mothering Sunday... but with never a glimmer of ill feeling, for no two hats were made alike.

Although fashionable at the time, my aunt would never use stuffed birds or ostrich feathers for her creations. She felt this was a cruel practice and a degradation of God's creatures.

Soon Aunt Hannah had another special 'line'. This was brought about by none other than the Mayoress, who requested a bridal headdress to be made for her only daughter who was marrying shortly. I shall always remember seeing the headdress for the first time. It was a filigree of ivory lace, adorned with honeysuckle and kissed by oyster pearls. To my childish imagination it was fit for a fairy princess.

After this many local girls went to the altar with shining countenances beneath a Hannah headdress. And I believe to this very day that their happiness stemmed from the fact that into each wedding veil my Aunt weaved a single silver hair from her own head. Although she had never married herself, such was her happiness that she believed God had truly laid His hand upon her head, and in this way she was passing his blessing on.

Many times she was asked why, now that the business was prospering, she didn't move to a larger establishment. But she was a great sentimentalist and clung on to Hannah's Hats in the High Street until the day she died.

Long afterwards, when I was grown-up, I visited the shop again. It was empty and forlorn-looking now, but

my sign, faded and almost illegible, still hung on the glass door. I paused, remembering, when a lady touched my shoulder.

"Excuse me, wasn't this a hat shop at one time?" she asked. "I wonder what became of that sweet little woman who made hats?"

I am ashamed to say I could only incline my head and walk on. My heart was too full to reply.

Aunt Hannah's Hats was first published in
This England magazine, *Summer 1994*

UNCLE JACK

As a child I was always very much in awe of my Uncle Jack. He was a mountain of a man with a booming voice that had me, a skinny pale-faced London kid, quaking in my shoes. It wasn't that he was unkind or uncaring but he just didn't understand children and thought they should be seen but not heard, which was the general attitude back in the 1930s.

Every summer my mother, father, brother and I would be invited to spend our holidays with Uncle Jack and Auntie Nan at Harbour Cottage at Gorleston-on-Sea, Norfolk. We were considered a bit like "poor relations" because Uncle was quite well off by our standards and owned Harbour Cottage, whilst Dad only earned two pounds ten shillings a week (old money) on the railway. So Mum had a struggle to feed and clothe us in our small rented terrace house in Walthamstow, E17.

I suppose Uncle and Auntie felt it was their duty to give us a seaside holiday every year away from the smoke of London and we were treated with a certain benevolence. Uncle Jack arranging trips on the Norfolk Broads and excursions to Cromer and Lowestoft with much aplomb, pointing out landmarks in his booming voice as if the whole of the East Coast belonged to him. Spending the holidays at Gorleston would have been idyllic for had I not felt so intimidated by Uncle Jack. I don't think my brother Ron felt the same way because he was seven years my senior and sensible enough to be allowed to pursue his own interests, which he did, wriggling out of the Norfolk Broads and Lowestoft trips and well out of Uncle Jack's way.

Every year I looked forward to seeing the wonderful sea. Dad had come from a seafaring family and I guess I had inherited their love of it. I loved its beautiful blue and green colours, its sparkle and its salty taste upon my lips. On our first evening's arrival at Uncle Jack's we would all journey by bus to Great Yarmouth and walk

along the sea front watching the Fisher Girls as they worked in their roughly made wooden sheds, gutting and packing herrings into huge barrels ready to send to their respective markets.

First they'd toss in a layer of fish, then a layer of salt and ice and carry on like this until the barrels were full to the brim and ready for batting down. The Fisher Girls, buxom red-armed women dressed in long aprons and headscarves, sang as they worked, their hands and knives flashing in the late evening sunlight. As their ribald laughter echoed all along the sea-front I would hold tight to my mothers' hand as we passed by, trembling with fear in case 'a little shrimp like me' as my Uncle put it, would be caught up and tossed into one of the barrels - but it was a lovely shivery fear, for I knew that really I was quite safe.

There was another happening in the holidays that I wasn't so keen on though. My mother was a firm believer in keeping one's bowels open, especially at holiday times, which in her eyes were disastrous in this respect. So half way through the week, whether needing it or not, I was given a double dose of that most evil of potions - senna-pods. Several pods were put into a cup and boiling water was poured over, then it was left to soak, ready for me to drink the next morning. However, if I was lucky and the opportunity arose, I'd quickly tip the horrible concoction down the sink or into the potted aspidistra that stood in Auntie Nan's front parlour. Once Uncle Jack walked into the room as I was 'watering' the aspidistra, but he said nothing although I'm certain he had seen me. For the rest of the day I kept a very low profile knowing I would get the back of my legs slapped if he told Auntie or my mother what I had done.

One thing both my brother and I liked was paddling in the sea. I used to wear 'paddlers' - rubber slippers that fitted tightly over one's feet to prevent the shingle from biting. Not that there was much shingle on Gorleston beach for it was always beautifully smooth

and fine and especially good for making sandcastles - though not so good when you ate your sandwiches. I remember Auntie Nan kept an empty shoebox in the corner of our bedroom so that any sand left in our shoes at the end of the day could be tipped in and not all over the bedroom floors. Even Mum and Dad had to adhere to these rules.

Then there was the Bertram Mills Circus at the Hippodrome, Yarmouth. Uncle Jack strongly disapproved of keeping wild animals in cages (in retrospect I now see that he wasn't such a hard man after all) and flatly refused to take Auntie Nan, so it was left to Mum and Dad to take us. I loved the clowns and the elephants but my brother Ron preferred the trapeze artists and the Stratosphere Girl. Dressed in a brilliantly sequined costume she would take her position on a small platform at the very top of a steel pole that stretched right up into the middle of the Big Top.

As a drum roll called for silence, all faces, young and old alike, turned upwards... waiting. You could have heard a pin drop as the spotlight played on her distant shimmering figure. Then suddenly she'd throw herself forward midst "oohs" and "aahs" of the audience and hurtle down at a great pace, seemingly hanging from an invisible wire by the skin of her teeth. As she gathered speed her whole body spun around like a sparkling Catherine Wheel. How pleased I was when she landed safely in the circus ring - but I can tell you it sent a shudder through me for a long time afterwards, especially when I visited the dentist!

Meal times were daunting to say the least. I was a poor eater, and because I was so skinny Uncle seemed bent on "fattening me up". Under his strict instructions Auntie Nan would fill my plate until I could hardly see over the top and always with an extra large helping of "greens" which I abhorred. Uncle's dinner would come on two plates, one full of succulent roast beef and crispy Yorkshire pudding, the other piled high with an

assortment of every kind of vegetable, plus a huge steaming golden-brown jacket potato. I never ceased to wonder how quickly he stowed all this food away into his large tummy with such relish, whilst I struggled uncomfortably with my meal under his critical eye, knowing I had to finish every last morsel.

I cannot say I was broken-hearted when Uncle Jack died. It was just after Christmas and we were back in Walthamstow when the telegram came from Auntie Nan begging us to attend his funeral. I was given the choice of staying with our neighbour Mrs Fletcher next door but I wanted to go with my parents and brother out of curiosity. I had no idea what a funeral would be like and anyway it was an excuse to see the lovely sea again. But the East Coast was bitterly cold in January, hardly recognisable as the same place where our previous summer had been spent. To make matters worse either Auntie or my mother put a stone hot water bottle in my bed and I badly stubbed my toe on it when I quickly thrust my feet down into the icy sheets. How I longed for my dear old soft and squashy hot water bottle that had been left at home.

Harbour Cottage looked quite drab without the sun shining on it and seemed strangely empty without Uncle Jack's presence. Wickedly I'd thought it might be better, but it turned out to be a miserable time for us all. My father was worried about having to take time off work and I was badly neglected by my mother who was too concerned about comforting Auntie Nan to bother much about me. Auntie had taken to trailing about the cottage most of the time with red-rimmed eyes murmuring "Now he knows the wonderful secret". I couldn't understand what she meant. What wonderful secret? Could it be anything to do with my tipping the senna-pods into the aspidistra?

The day of the funeral arrived, cold and bleak. We all stood watching the coffin being lowered into the ground. I just couldn't believe Uncle Jack was inside, it

looked much too small and shallow to house his huge body. I wondered if part of his gigantic tummy had been sliced off and slipped down the sides of the coffin until all of him fitted neatly in like a jigsaw puzzle. It wasn't until years later I leaned that you had to be measured by the undertaker to make sure you fitted into your last abode. Auntie Nan moved forward and dropped a single red rose on top of the varnished box and I had the grace to shed a tear. After all, Uncle Jack had probably always had my best interests at heart - but secret or no secret, even if he had known about the senna-pods, he would never be able to tell Auntie or my mother now.

You Raise Me Up

A LITTLE BIT OF JESUS

There's a little bit of Jesus
In everyone we meet
So let us try remember this
When next a soul we greet.

We know that human beings
Are a mixture ......good and bad
But if we seek to find the good
The good's there to be had.

All of us can make mistakes
It's not for us to judge
We can only keep our faith
And try to show our love.

For God has given all a chance
By sending down His Son
To spread the beauty of His soul
And enrich us, everyone.

So if we try to live God's way
Our lives can be made sweet
For there's a little bit of Jesus
In everyone we meet.

CARES

Take your cares to Jesus
He will see you through
Your trials and tribulations
And things that worry you.
Let His arms uplift you
And fold you to His breast
Leave your cares with Jesus
He knows what is best.

WITH YOU

Whatever I've got to do today Lord
I'm going to do it with you.
Whatever tasks you set before me
I can manage... if you are there too.

By myself I am nothing
On my own I could never "touch start"
But everything I can aspire to
If I carry you in my heart.

In life we find many pitfalls
Things tempt us and bring us down low
But you Lord will keep us from falling
If we follow the path that you show.

So today Lord with joy I will cherish
The spirit of you in my heart
Certain that if I should stumble
You'll help me to make a new start.

I know that with you close beside me
There's nothing that I cannot do
The hardest of tasks I can manage
As long as I'm walking with you.

TO BE A CHRISTIAN

I'd like to be a Christian
Steadfastly strong and wise
I'd like to feel the power of prayer
Each time I close my eyes.

But I am just a floating soul
Who feels and cares and cries
And when I see a suffering
... I can only sympathise.

I'd like to utter soothing words
To take away the pain
And wonder what the Lord would say
If He were here again.

But then, if you're a Christian
His spirit will be within
And He'll help you with those healing words
As soon as you begin.

THE WONDERFUL GIFT

God was very disappointed in us. He had given us this marvelous world but what did we do? We were greedy and sinful and it seemed, bent on our own destruction.

God felt like ending it all because of men's evil - but then he thought "I'll give them one more chance, I will send down my own son in the guise of a man, to be an example for all to follow." And so Jesus, the most wonderful man who ever lived, was born.

But because Jesus was such a perfect human, many people rejected him. They didn't understand him and couldn't identify with him, for he was without sin. Jesus lived for 33 years doing many miraculous things. He fed the poor, healed the sick and never put a foot wrong. But the priests and elders of the time were not pleased and in the end they let the people have their way - and Jesus was crucified.

Jesus could have saved himself if he had only asked God to release him but he knew that if he did so he would not be fulfilling his duty to his Father or to us. Instead he allowed himself to be led away and cruelly put to death on the cross.

If Jesus had not died this way, there would have been no Holy Spirit, for when his soul was raised to Heaven all the spiritual power that had enabled him to live such a perfect life on earth, flowed from him down to us - and still lives within us today if we want it. It is our choice.

We can be the biggest of sinners and the most miserable of men but the moment we invite Jesus into our lives we become the inheritors of the Kingdom of Heaven and the recipients of the everlasting life.

How can we refuse such a wonderful gift?

THE SOUL

The soul is like a diamond... neglect it and it will cloud over like a piece of dirty glass.

Polish it, keep it clean and free from evil thoughts and it will shine brighter than God's brightest star.

Dear Jesus, You are the loveliest person I have ever known and You are with me until the end of time... throughout all eternity.

Thank you.

THE CRUCIFIX

A blonde with over-shadowed eyes
Stood on the corner there
Looking first this way then that
Fingering peroxide hair.
And as she moved I caught a glint
Of something bright that shone
Against the bareness of her neck,
Something I thought was wrong
A Crucifix!... how could it be,
That she should ever dare
His sign was not for folks like her,
T'was not for her to wear.
But wait... dear Lord, will you forgive
As I am such a fool
And did not stop to realise
YOUR sign is meant for all

THANK YOU GOD

Thank you God for this lovely day
Help me to use it in a proper way.
Don't let me spoil it 'neath a frown
No matter how things get me down.

Help me spread the joy I'll feel
Just by trying to do your will.
Perhaps I'll reach somebody who
Hasn't yet been saved by you.

We all need faith to quell our fear
When the dark clouds gather near.
Without your help we'd all be lost
But you dear God have paid the cost.

By sending down your Son from high
That we might live... and never die.
So let us lift our hearts and pray
Thank you God for this lovely day.

MRS HAINES RETURNS HOME

Mrs Haines passed the church without even a glance in its direction. There had been a time when she'd stopped in awe at all churches, admiring their stained glass windows and meditating on the good works that evolved from within. But that had been a long time ago - three years to be exact; for it had been three years ago when her husband and teenage son had been killed in a car crash at the Riley Crossroads, almost in the shadow of the spire of the Parish Church where, until then, they had worshipped as a family every Sunday.

Apart from attending Frank and Raymond's funerals, she'd not set foot inside a church since. In her anger she had turned away from God for how could He have let this thing happen to her? Hadn't she been a good Christian, going to church every Sunday and trying to keep His commandments? Yet there was Violet Saunders who lived in the "posh" house down the road and never had a good word to say for anyone, seemingly blessed with all good things although she led her husband and children a dog's life.

No," Mrs Haines muttered to herself, feeling the rheumatism in her knees give a twinge as she climbed the steps of the shabby flatlet house in which she now lived. "There just wasn't any justice."

Frank and she had had a nice little house once, perhaps not on such a grand scale as the Saunders who'd lived in the same road, but they'd been a happy, contented family thriving in perfect harmony until the day God had seen fit to end it all. After that she had sold the house and furniture, unable to bear the pain of it all - unable to go into her son's empty room where he'd spent his boyhood or look at the comfortable old armchair where Frank had rested when returning from his work every evening. One by one she'd dropped her

church-going friends; even avoiding them in the street to save the embarrassment of being asked why she no longer attended church. Finally she'd moved away from the district and was now living alone in a tiny flatlet she called "home".

Mrs Haines plonked her shopping bag down on the rickety chair and plugged in the electric kettle. A cup of tea always cheered her up when she was feeling low... and today hadn't been a good day for her. Everything in the shops was so expensive - and her widow's pension hardly went anywhere. Nearly all the money she'd got from the house was gone although she'd augmented it by taking on casual work here and there. However, the time had come, she felt, when she'd really have to get something permanent if she didn't want to get into debt.

Sipping her tea she ran her eye down the situations vacant column of the local newspaper she'd brought with her - not that there was much for people in her age group - but suddenly her eye caught one advertisement that sounded promising

Kindly lady required for light
domestic duties. Age immaterial.
Used to working on own initiative.
Apply: Mrs Vee, Woodley Court

Well she certainly could work on her own initiative; in fact preferred it. She made a ring around the advert. She was too tired to trudge down to the town again now - but she <u>might</u> go tomorrow... just to see.

* * * * *

"Yes, I'm Mrs. Vee." A grey haired lady in her early sixties answered the door. "Come in my dear," she invited after Mrs Haines had stated her reason for

calling. "You look just the sort of person I require but you'd better give me a few details about yourself before I tell you what the work involves."

Mrs Haines sketched out a few details for Mrs Vee who seemed quite satisfied.

"Well dear, the work needing doing isn't in this house but just down the road. Wait until I slip on my coat and I'll take you along".

Mrs Haines was surprised - and a little disappointed for she had taken an instant liking to Mrs Vee and the house. But she waited patiently in the comfortable lounge, enjoying the homely surroundings. She supposed Mrs Vee was a woman of property - maybe she owned a flatlet house and needed someone to "do" the hall and staircases! So many of these large Victorian houses were being let out in flatlets today. But she wasn't prepared for what happened next, for Mrs Vee, chatting kindly all the time, walked her steadily down the road then stopped looking up lovingly at... of all places... a church! Mrs Haines's heart almost stopped beating as she was led up the steps and through the heavy arched door.

"Yes, it's very beautiful isn't it?" Mrs Vee said softly, mistaking her hesitation to be one of awe. "My husband is the Vicar here but he doesn't seem to be able to get a reliable cleaner. He's not fussy but wants someone he can trust, a special person who might grow to love the church as much as he does."

Mrs Haines drew back.

"I thought I'd try to find that special person for him as I'm generally right with my intuition... and I'm sure you're the one."

Mrs Haines swallowed, at a loss for words. In a daze she heard the Vicar's wife pointing out the work that needed doing in the church. "Now my dear, what do you think?" Her calm grey eyes questioned Mrs Haines's face.

"I...I...I'm not quite sure. I'd like to think it over," Mrs

Haines blurted out in utter confusion. Somehow she felt that things were being taken out of her hands; that there was a force working against her wishes. "Would it be all right if I give you a ring in the morning, and let you know what I decide?"

A flicker of disappointment touched Mrs Vee's kind eyes but she nodded, taking a card with her telephone number from her handbag and handing it to Mrs Haines who took her leave almost apologetically.

* * * * *

After spending the night tossing and turning, Mrs Haines finally made up her mind. After all, she needed a job badly... no need to think about her surroundings whilst she worked. Dusting and cleaning were the same whether it was ordinary furniture or church pews. Anyway, she'd give it a try and keep herself impartial to it all. Mrs Vee was delighted when Mrs Haines phoned to say she would start that morning. The church would be open, Mrs Vee said, and all the cleaning materials were kept in a small cupboard in the vestibule.

After putting on her overall Mrs Haines began methodically to dust and polish. Soon she found herself relaxing in the peaceful atmosphere. The noise of the traffic outside faded into the background and soon she was absorbed in her task and taking joy in her work... something she hadn't done for a long time. One of the parishioners came and left a beautiful bunch of mauve and white asters and she found herself arranging them in a large brass container, which she'd just polished. She almost found herself humming *Onward Christian Soldiers* but it was as she arose from straightening up one of the hassocks that a sudden gleam caught her eye... the gloss of a shining crucifix that hung on the wall nearby.

The suffering face of Christ made her draw nearer... and it was then that all the bitterness in her heart

disappeared, for what was her suffering compared with His and who was she to cause Him more pain by turning away. Suddenly she was down on her knees praying for forgiveness, and as she did so a wonderful feeling of peace and well being overwhelmed her... for Mrs Haines had returned home at last.

Lightning Source UK Ltd.
Milton Keynes UK
UKOW030802210412

191232UK00002B/8/P

9 781907 897016